Identifying Chincoteague Ponies 2020

Cover photo: Surfer's Riptide, 12/31/2019.

**Other books from
Jennie's Music Room Books**

Nicio and Cedar Fire
Legends of Two-Legs
Identifying Chincoteague Ponies [2017]
Identifying Chincoteague Ponies 2018
Identifying Chincoteague Ponies 2019

Text and illustrations copyright © 2020
by Gina Aguilera

Jennie's Music Room Books
4241 Filmore St
Chincoteague Island, VA 23336

ISBN: 978-0-9842392-8-3

Library of Congress Control Number: 2020902199

Contents

Preface

Preface

About This Book

The primary purpose of this book is to aid in the identification of individual members of the feral herd of horses known as Chincoteague ponies. These ponies reside on the southern Virginia end of Assateague Island. There is a completely separate herd at the northern Maryland end of the island know as Assateague horses. The Maryland herd is not included in this book.

This book is the work of one person. The author took the photos, drew the drawings, collected the data, formatted the pages and published the book.

There will be times when you will not be able to positively identify an individual using one resource. Animals with solid coats and very light pintos can be hard to identify. Colors appear differently depending on the season, weather, and lighting conditions. Long hair in the winter may obscure brands. Mud can cover legs. Manes blow around.

The author recommends that when in doubt, search the internet. She starts with the Chincoteague Pony Pedigree Database at chincoteaguepedigrees.com. Besides interesting geneology information, there are links to other web sites with photo galleries and band information. Another method is to post pictures and ask in any of the various Facebook pony groups, like I Love Chincoteague Ponies!

To report errors or to make suggestions for next year's book, please message me through my Facebook page - Chincoteague Pony Names.

Organization

Ponies are grouped alphabetically by color. **Bay**: Any dark colored horse with black points*. Colors range from shades of red to very dark brown. **Black**: An all black horse including points*. **Buckskin**: Any light colored horse with black/brown points*. Colors range from very light cream to yellow, tan, or gold. **Chestnut**: A reddish brown horse. Colors range from light red to deep mahogany. **Palomino**: A pale horse with white mane and tail. Colors range from cream to golden.

*points: legs, muzzle, mane and tail, and tips of ears

Each color is divided into 3 sections. **Solid:** A horse with no white markings on the body other than face and legs. **Comparison Chart**: Additional characteristics that might aid in identifying a solid horse. **Pinto**: A horse with white markings on the body other than face and legs. Any horse could have white on the face and legs.

Alphabetical by name, brand, and stallion indexes are included. The alphabetical index includes official names and popular nicknames.

There is also an family index which shows the relationships of the current living members of the herd. For more detailed pedigrees, refer to the Chincoteague Pony Pedigree Database at chincoteaguepedigrees.com.

Bay

Bay Girl

Fluffy
mare   birth year: 1999   brand: none
WITCH DOCTOR x WILD ISLAND ORCHID

Brown eyes.

Notes:

_____
_____
_____
_____
_____
_____
_____
_____
_____
_____
_____

4

Bay Girl

Bay

Daisey

mare   birth year: 2004   brand: none
CINNAMON HOLOGRAM x MERRY TEAPOT'S HIGH BID

Brown eyes. Sold at the 2004 auction and donated back to CVFD in 2012 by auction buyer Don Thornton. Alternate sire: Witch Doctor, Alternate dam: Wild Island Orchid.

Notes:

_____

_____

_____

_____

_____

_____

_____

_____

_____

_____

_____

Daisey

Bay

Doc's Bay Dream

Bay Dream
mare   birth year: 2018   brand: 18
EFFIE'S PAPA BEAR x DOCTOR AMRIEN

Brown eyes. Auction price: $7,500. First seen April 5, 2018. Buyback donator: Dan and Abby Davis family, Darcy and Steve Cole, and friends of Capt Dan.

Notes:

Doc's Bay Dream

Bay

Effie's Papa Bear

Poseidon's Fury, Hoppy
stallion   birth year: 2007   brand: 07
SOCKETT TO ME x MERMAID

Brown eyes. Auction price: $7,500. Born April 9, 2007. Buyback donator: Stephanie Guerlain.

Notes:

_____

_____

_____

_____

_____

_____

_____

_____

_____

_____

_____

Effie's Papa Bear

Bay

Little Dolphin

Neptune
stallion   birth year: 2008   brand: 08
RAINBOW WARRIOR x LANDRIE'S GEORGIA PEACH

Brown eyes. Born May 14, 2008. King Neptune. Donated back by raffle winner.

Notes:

_____

_____

_____

_____

_____

_____

_____

_____

_____

_____

_____

Little Dolphin

Bay

Pappy's Pony

mare   birth year: 2003   brand: 03
OCEAN STAR x ISLAND STAR

Brown eyes. Auction price: $6,600. Born July 16, 2003. Alternate sire: Witch Doctor. Buyback donator: Stepp family.

Notes:

_____

_____

_____

_____

_____

_____

_____

_____

_____

_____

Pappy's Pony

Bay

Pony Ladies' Sweet Surprise

Lady
mare   birth year: 2004   brand: 04
GUNNER'S MOON x SWEET INSPIRATION

Brown eyes. Auction price: $3,150. Born May 2, 2004. Buyback donator: Buyback Babes.

Notes:

_____

_____

_____

_____

_____

_____

_____

_____

_____

_____

Pony Ladies' Sweet Surprise

Bay

Thunderbolt

stallion   birth year: 2018   brand: 18
CHIEF GOLDEN EAGLE X BLING BLING

*Brown eyes. First seen
May 14, 2018. Donated
back to CVFC.*

Notes:

_____

_____

_____

_____

_____

_____

_____

_____

_____

_____

Thunderbolt

Bay

Two Teagues Taco

Taco
mare   birth year: 2005   brand: 05
Witch Doctor x Wild Island Orchid

Brown eyes. Auction price: $5,000. Born July 12, 2005. Buyback donator: Myfe Moore.

Notes:

_____

_____

_____

_____

_____

_____

_____

_____

_____

_____

_____

_____

Two Teagues Taco

Bay

Unci

mare   birth year: 1995   brand: none
(UNKNOWN) X (UNKNOWN)

Brown eyes. Swayback.

swayback

Notes:

_____

_____

_____

_____

_____

_____

swayback

_____

_____

_____

_____

_____

Unci

Bay

Jean Bonde's Bayside Angel

Angel

mare   birth year: 2015   brand: 15, partial

SOCKETT TO ME x LEAH'S BAYSIDE ANGEL

Brown eyes. Auction price: $6,400. Born April 22, 2015. Buyback donator: Buyback Babes.

Notes:

_____

_____

_____

_____

_____

_____

_____

_____

_____

_____

_____

Jean Bonde's Bayside Angel

Bay

Leah's Bayside Angel

mare   birth year: 1999   brand: unreadable
OCEAN STAR x SUMMER BREEZE

Brown eyes. Born July 1999.

Notes:

_____

_____

_____

_____

_____

_____

_____

_____

_____

_____

_____

Leah's Bayside Angel

Bay

Tawny Treasure

mare   birth year: 2017   brand: 17
EFFIE'S PAPA BEAR x ISLE TREASURE

Brown eyes. Auction
price: $7,100. First seen
June 14, 2017. Buyback
donator: Wanda and
George Panos.

Notes:

_____

_____

_____

_____

_____

_____

_____

_____

_____

_____

_____

Tawny Treasure

Bay

Dakota Sky's Cody Two Socks

Cody
mare   birth year: 2005   brand: 05, partial

Copper Moose x Stevenson's Dakota Sky

Brown eyes. Auction price: $5,000. Born May 28, 2005. Buyback donator: Catherine Young.

Notes:

_____

_____

_____

_____

_____

_____

_____

_____

_____

_____

Dakota Sky's Cody Two Socks

Bay

Bling Bling

mare   birth year: 2014   brand: 15
TORNADO'S LEGACY x UNFORGETTABLE 2001

Brown eyes. Auction price: $4,600. Born August 24, 2014. Auctioned in 2015 as a yearling.

Notes:

Bling Bling

Bay Comparision Chart

Name	Pg #	Brand	Mane	Face
Bay Girl	4		left	
Bling Bling	32	15	left	star
Daisey	6		right	
Dakota Sky's Cody Two Socks	30	05, partial	right	star
Doc's Bay Dream	8	18	left	
Effie's Papa Bear	10	07	left	
Jean Bonde's Bayside Angel	24	15, partial	left	star
Leah's Bayside Angel	26	unreadable	right	star
Little Dolphin	12	08	right	
Pappy's Pony	14	03	right	
Pony Ladies' Sweet Surprise	16	04	left	
Tawny Treasure	28	17	right	star
Thunderbolt	18	18	right	
Two Teagues Taco	20	05	left	
Unci	22		right	

NOTES

Left & right refers to the animal's left & right.

Mane: **left** = falls to the left **right** = falls to the right **split** = significant portion falls on left and right

Legs				Notable Details
R F	R B	L F	L B	
	sock	sock	sock	
	sock		sock	upper half of 5 is gone
				stallion; very dark mane and tail
				top of 1 in brand is obscured
				stallion; small statute
				stallion; 8 looks like a 0
				swayback

R F = right front   **R B** = right back **L F** = left front   **L B** = left back
sock = white well below the knee   **stocking** = white near and above the knee

baldface = white covers most of the face   **blaze** = white streak running down the length
of the face   **snip** = white spot on the muzzle   **star** = white spot on the forehead

Bay Pinto

Rosie's Teapot

mare   birth year: 2013   brand: 13
AJAX x MOLLY'S ROSEBUD

Brown eyes. Born Fall 2013.

Notes:

_____

_____

_____

_____

_____

_____

_____

_____

_____

_____

_____

Rosie's Teapot

Bay Pinto

Scarlett's Little Bee

Little Bee, Bee
mare   birth year: 2019   brand: 19
KEN x MAY'S GRAND SLAM

Brown eyes. Auction price: $10,000. First seen June 23, 2019. Alternate sire: Archer's Gambit. Buyback donator: Debra Evalds.

Notes:

_____

_____

_____

_____

_____

_____

_____

_____

_____

_____

_____

Scarlett's Little Bee

Bay Pinto

CLG Maureen's Misty Moon

Misty Moon, Maureen
mare   birth year: 2019   brand: 19
DON LEONARD STUD II X WINTER MOON

Brown eyes. Auction price: $15,000. First seen April 8, 2019. Buyback donator: Chincoteague Legacy Group. Great great great great grandfoal of Misty.

Notes:

_____

_____

_____

_____

_____

_____

_____

_____

_____

_____

_____

CLG Maureen's Misty Moon

Bay Pinto

Good Golly Miss Molly

Molly
mare   birth year: 2019   brand: 19
Tornado's Legacy x A Splash of Freckles

Brown eyes. Auction price: $7,400. First seen May 27, 2019.

Notes:

_____

_____

_____

_____

_____

_____

_____

_____

_____

_____

_____

_____

_____

Good Golly Miss Molly

Bay Pinto

Summer Breeze

Cee Cee, Breezy
mare   birth year: 2006 brand: none
MIRACLE MAN X BINKY'S BREEZE

Brown eyes. Born August 2006. Not auctioned, no buyback donator.

Notes:

_____

_____

_____

_____

_____

_____

_____

_____

_____

_____

Summer Breeze

Bay Pinto

Ella of Assateague

Ella
mare   birth year: 2000   brand: 00
CINNAMON HOLOGRAM X FOXY ASSET

Brown eyes. Born July 2000. Buyback donator: Cara Rosenbaum.

Notes:

_____

_____

_____

_____

_____

_____

_____

_____

_____

_____

_____

Bay Pinto

Ella of Assateague

Bay Pinto

Doctor Amrien

Doc
mare   birth year: 2014   brand: 14
WILD THING x DAKOTA SKY'S CODY TWO SOCKS

Brown eyes. Born
September 1, 2014.
Buyback donator: Dan
and Abby Davis family.

Notes:

_____

_____

_____

_____

_____

_____

_____

_____

_____

_____

_____

Doctor Amrien

Bay Pinto

White Saddle

mare   birth year: 2013   brand: 13
Witch Doctor x Wild Island Orchid

Brown eyes. Auction price: $4,100. Born April 5, 2013. Buyback donator: Joan Bradley.

Notes:

_____

_____

_____

_____

_____

_____

_____

_____

_____

_____

White Saddle

Bay Pinto

Miracle's Natural Beauty

Natural Beauty
mare   birth year: 2009   brand: 09
Miracle Man x Natural Innocence

Brown eyes. Auction price: $3,100. Born April 30, 2009. Buyback donator: Debbie and Landrie Folsom.

Notes:

_____

_____

_____

_____

_____

_____

_____

_____

_____

_____

_____

Miracle's Natural Beauty

Bay Pinto

May's Grand Slam

May
mare   birth year: 2012   brand: 12
MIRACLE MAN x SPANISH ANGEL

Brown eyes. Auction price: $4,700. Born April 23, 2012. Buyback donator: Loveland family.

Notes:

May's Grand Slam

Bay Pinto

Tunie

Queenie
mare   birth year: 2003   brand: 03
WILLIE'S MAJESTIC DREAMER x SEASIDE

*Brown eyes. Born
July 7, 2003. Queen
Neptune. Donated back
by raffle winner.*

Notes:

Tunie

Bay Pinto

Wendy's Carolina Girl

Carolina Girl
mare   birth year: 2018   brand: 18
MAVERICK x ESSIE

Brown eyes. Auction price: $6,500. First seen May 14, 2018. Buyback donator: Wendy Sloan.

Notes:

_____

_____

_____

_____

_____

_____

_____

_____

_____

_____

_____

Wendy's Carolina Girl

Bay Pinto

Ajax

stallion   birth year: 2007   brand: 07, partial
YANKEE SPIRIT x FOXY ASSET

Brown eyes. Auction price: $6,600. Born April 6, 2007. Buyback donator: Cara Rosenbaum.

Notes:

Ajax

Bay Pinto

MissMe

mare   birth year: 2017   brand: 17
AJAX x MIRACLE'S NATURAL BEAUTY

Brown eyes. Auction price: $13,500. First seen May 19, 2017.

Notes:

MissMe

Bay Pinto

Babe

mare   birth year: 1994   brand: 94, partial
WITCH DOCTOR x WILD FIRE

Brown eyes. Auction
price: $850. Born
July 1994. Buyback
donator: The Giddings
Family: Richard
Giddings, Norman
& Janet Giddings,
and grandchildren
Casie, Westley, Lauren,
Kaitlyn, Sarah, Niki,
Christy, Jessica, &
Emmalee.

Notes:

Babe

Bay Pinto

Millennium Midnight

Oreo
mare   birth year: 2000   brand: none
MIRACLE MAN x CHANTILLY LACE

Brown eyes. Donated to CVFC December 2018.

Notes:

_____

_____

_____

_____

_____

_____

_____

_____

_____

_____

_____

Millennium Midnight

Bay Pinto

Norman Rockwell Giddings

Norm, Rocky
stallion   birth year: 2018   brand: none
ARCHER'S GAMBIT X BABE

Brown eyes. Auction price: $4,000. First seen May 1, 2018. Donated to the CVFC October 2019. Tested homozygous for tobiano.

Notes:

Norman Rockwell Giddings

Bay Pinto

Sissy

mare   birth year: 2019   brand: 19
Effie's Papa Bear x Splash

Brown eyes. Auction price: $16,000. First seen April 1, 2019.

Notes:

Sissy

Bay Pinto

Rainbow Warrior

Napolean
stallion   birth year: 1997   brand: none
(UNKNOWN) X (UNKNOWN)

Brown eyes.

Notes:

_____

_____

_____

_____

_____

_____

_____

_____

_____

_____

Rainbow Warrior

Bay Pinto

Destiny Feathering Spirit

Destiny
mare   birth year: 2002   brand: none
Courtney's Boy x Vixen

Brown eyes. Born August 2002. Buyback donator: Joann Rome and Ginny Zlevitch.

Notes:

_____

_____

_____

_____

_____

_____

_____

_____

_____

_____

_____

_____

Destiny Feathering Spirit

Bay Pinto

Sweetheart

mare   birth year: 2011   brand: unreadable
WILD BILL x SCOTTY ET

Brown eyes. Auction price: $4,650. Born April 18, 2011.

Notes:

_____

_____

_____

_____

_____

_____

_____

_____

_____

_____

_____

Sweetheart

Bay Pinto

Henry's Hidalgo

stallion   birth year: 2017   brand: 17
WILD THING x THETIS

Brown eyes. Auction price: $8,900. First seen May 14, 2017. Buyback donator: Arthur Leonard.

Notes:

_____

_____

_____

_____

_____

_____

_____

_____

_____

_____

_____

Henry's Hidalgo

Bay Pinto

Splash

Danny's Girl
mare   birth year: 2014   brand: 14
WILD THING x SUMMER BREEZE

Brown eyes. Auction price: $7,100. Buyback donator: Beers Family.

Notes:

Splash

Bay Pinto

Grandma's Dream

mare   birth year: 2013   brand: 13
WILD THING x GALADRIEL

Brown eyes. Auction price: $4,600. Born May 7, 2013. Buyback donator: Frances Bidoglio.

Notes:

_____

_____

_____

_____

_____

_____

_____

_____

_____

_____

_____

Grandma's Dream

Bay Pinto

Loveland's Secret Feather

Secret, Feather
mare   birth year: 2012   brand: 12
Wild Thing x Galadriel

Brown eyes. Auction
price: $7,200. Born
May 1, 2012. Buyback
donator: Loveland
family.

Notes:

_____

_____

_____

_____

_____

_____

_____

_____

_____

_____

_____

_____

Loveland's Secret Feather

Bay Pinto

Wild Thing

stallion   birth year: 1997   brand: none
HURRICANE x JUST MY STYLE

Brown eyes.

Notes:

_____

_____

_____

_____

_____

_____

_____

_____

_____

_____

_____

Wild Thing

Bay Pinto

Chickadee

mare   birth year: 2013   brand: 13
Courtney's Boy x Black Star

Brown eyes. Auction price: $5,000. Born April 15, 2013. Buyback donator: Janey Beer.

Notes:

_____

_____

_____

_____

_____

_____

_____

_____

_____

_____

_____

_____

Chickadee

Bay Pinto

Wildest Dreams

mare   birth year: 2008   brand: 08
MIRACLE MAN x NATURAL INNOCENCE

Brown eyes. Auction price: $7,200. Born April 28, 2008.

Notes:

Wildest Dreams

Bay Pinto

Black Star

mare   birth year: 1998   brand: none
WITCH DOCTOR x RAP THE WIND

Brown eyes. Born
August 1998.

Notes:

_____

_____

_____

_____

_____

_____

_____

_____

_____

_____

Black Star

Bay Pinto

Marguerite of Chincoteague

mare   birth year: 2013   brand: 13

Archer's Gambit x Miracle's Natural Beauty

Brown eyes. Auction price: $5,800. Born April 25, 2013. Alternate sire: Tornado's Legacy. Buyback donator: Ellen Wycoski.

Notes:

_____

_____

_____

_____

_____

_____

_____

_____

_____

_____

_____

Marguerite of Chincoteague

Bay Pinto

Shy Anne

Half n Half
mare   birth year: 1999   brand: none
HOT AIR BALLOON x SUNSHINE

Brown eyes. Born July 1999. Buyback donator: McCaskill family.

Notes:

_____
_____
_____
_____
_____
_____
_____

_____
_____
_____
_____

Bay Pinto

Shy Anne

Bay Pinto

Fifteen Friends of Freckles

Freckles
mare   birth year: 2006   brand: 06
NORTH STAR X MARK'S ISLAND LIBERTY

One blue, one brown eye. Auction price: $7,500. Born May 15, 2006. Buyback donator: Buyback Babes.

Notes:

_____
_____
_____
_____
_____
_____
_____

_____
_____
_____
_____

Fifteen Friends of Freckles

Bay Pinto

Skylark

mare   birth year: 2011   brand: none
WILD THING x FOXY ASSET

Brown eyes. Auction price: $4,000. Born May 24, 2011. Buyback donator: Kathleen Cahall.

Notes:

_____

_____

_____

_____

_____

_____

_____

_____

_____

_____

_____

Skylark

Bay Pinto

Scotty ET

ET

mare   birth year: 2002   brand: 02, partial

Attitude x Black Star

Brown eyes. Auction price: $4,300. Born May 5, 2002. Buyback donator: Jean Bonde.

Notes:

_____

_____

_____

_____

_____

_____

_____

_____

_____

_____

_____

Scotty ET

Bay Pinto

Winter Moon

Moon
mare   birth year: 2012   brand: none
CYCLONE II x HEART OF THE BAY

One blue, one brown
eye. Born January 12,
2012. Donated to CVFC
March 2018. Great
great great grandfoal
of Misty.

Notes:

_____

_____

_____

_____

_____

_____

_____

_____

_____

_____

Winter Moon

Bay Pinto

Sky Dancer

mare   birth year: 2019   brand: 19
Ajax x Skylark

Blue eyes. Auction price: $6,400. First seen July 13, 2019. Buyback donator: Liane Pfeiffer.

Notes:

Sky Dancer

Bay Pinto

Summer

mare   birth year: 2015   brand: none
WH Nightwind x Justa Kickamazoo

Brown eyes. Donated to the CVFC March 2018. Great Great Great Grandfoal of Misty.

Notes:

_____

_____

_____

_____

_____

_____

_____

_____

_____

_____

_____

Summer

Bay Pinto

Seaside Miracle

mare   birth year: 2011   brand: F

MIRACLE MAN x SEASIDE

Brown eyes. Auction price: $4,600. Born May 7, 2011.

Notes:

_____

_____

_____

_____

_____

_____

_____

_____

_____

_____

_____

_____

Seaside Miracle

Bay Pinto

A Splash of Freckles

Splash of Freckles
mare   birth year: 2011   brand: unreadable
DON LEONARD STUD x FIFTEEN FRIENDS OF FRECKLES

Brown eyes. Auction price: $6,700. Born June 25, 2011. Buyback donator: Buyback Babes.

Notes:

_____

_____

_____

_____

_____

_____

_____

_____

_____

_____

_____

A Splash of Freckles

Bay Pinto

Maverick

stallion   birth year: 2013   brand: 14
WILD THING x WITCH KRAFT

Brown eyes. Auction
price: $12,700. Buyback
donator: Catherine
Miller. Born December
2013, sold at 2014
auction.

Notes:

_____

_____

_____

_____

_____

_____

_____

_____

_____

_____

_____

Maverick

Bay Pinto

Got Milk

Anna

mare   birth year: 2000   brand: none

WITCH DOCTOR x WATERKOLOR

Brown eyes. Born October 8, 2000. Alternate sire: Top Gun.

Notes:

_____

_____

_____

_____

_____

_____

_____

_____

_____

_____

_____

Got Milk

Bay Pinto

Heide's Sky

mare   birth year: 2017 brand: none
KEN X FIFTEEN FRIENDS OF FRECKLES

Blue eyes. First seen August 21, 2017. Buyback donator: Cindy Wolfe.

Notes:

_____

_____

_____

_____

_____

_____

_____

_____

_____

_____

_____

Heide's Sky

Black

CLG Ember

Ember
mare   birth year: 2018   brand: 18
SURFER'S RIPTIDE x BLACK PEARL

Brown eyes. Auction price: $11,000. First seen April 29, 2018. Buyback donator: Chincoteague Legacy Group.

Notes:

CLG Ember

Black

Dexter's Midnight Runner

Dexie
mare   birth year: 2019   brand: 19
MAVERICK X BLACK PEARL

Brown eyes. Auction price: $17,500. First seen June 5, 2019.

Notes:

_____
_____
_____
_____
_____
_____
_____
_____
_____
_____

Dexter's Midnight Runner

Black

Talia/Evan's Angel

Evan's Angel, Talia
mare   birth year: 2017   brand: 17
MAVERICK x SURFIN' CHANTEL

Brown eyes. Auction price: $7,400. First seen May 21, 2017. Buyback donator: Greg and Lissa St. Claire.

Notes:

_____

_____

_____

_____

_____

_____

_____

_____

_____

_____

_____

Talia/Evan's Angel

Black

Milly Sue

mare   birth year: 2017   brand: 17
SURFER'S RIPTIDE x LEAH'S BAYSIDE ANGEL

Brown eyes. Auction price: $9,000. First seen April 29, 2017.

Notes:

126

Milly Sue

CLG Surfer's Blue Moon

Blue, Blue Moon, Surfer's Blue Moon
mare   birth year: 2015   brand: 15
SURFER DUDE x GOT MILK

Blue eyes. Auction price: $25,000. Born April 27, 2015. Buyback donator: Chincoteague Legacy Group.

Notes:

CLG Surfer's Blue Moon

Black Comparision Chart

Name	Pg #	Brand	Mane	Face
Ace's Black Tie Affair	132	07	right	
CLG Ember	120	18	left	
CLG Surfer's Blue Moon	128	15	even	baldface
Dexter's Midnight Runner	122	19	right	
Milly Sue	126	17	right	
Talia/Evan's Angel	124	17	right	

NOTES

Ace's Black Tie Affair is included here even though he is technically a pinto. His markings are so minimal that he is routinely wrongly identified as solid black.

Left & right refers to the animal's left & right.

Mane: left = falls to the left **right** = falls to the right **split** = significant portion falls on left and right

Legs				Notable Details
R F	**R B**	**L F**	**L B**	
sock	stocking	sock	stocking	stallion; small upside heart behind left front leg
sock	sock	sock	sock	blue eyes
sock		sock	sock	7 in brand easily mistaken for 1

R F = right front   **R B** = right back   **L F** = left front   **L B** = left back
sock = white well below the knee   **stocking** = white near and above the knee

baldface = white covers most of the face   **blaze** = white streak running down the length of the face   **snip** = white spot on the muzzle   **star** = white spot on the forehead

Black Pinto

Ace's Black Tie Affair

Ace
stallion   birth year: 2007   brand: 07
CENTAUR X SUSIE Q

Brown eyes. Auction price: $9,500. Born May 1, 2007. Buyback donator: Folsom family.

Notes:

_____

_____

_____

_____

_____

_____

_____

_____

_____

_____

Ace's Black Tie Affair

Black Pinto

Poco's Starry Night

Starry Night, Cash
mare   birth year: 2012   brand: 12
DON LEONARD STUD x POCO LATTE PW

Brown eyes. Auction price: $6,700. Born April 9, 2012. Buyback donator: Buyback Babes.

Notes:

_____

_____

_____

_____

_____

_____

_____

_____

_____

_____

_____

Poco's Starry Night

Black Pinto

Pixie Dust

mare   birth year: 2014   brand: 14
ACE'S BLACK TIE AFFAIR X ANGEL WINGS

Brown eyes. Born August 29, 2014. Buyback donator: Brett Emmerson.

Notes:

_____

_____

_____

_____

_____

_____

_____

_____

_____

_____

_____

Pixie Dust

Black Pinto

Gracey

mare   birth year: 2013   brand: 13
Sockett To Me x Leah's Bayside Angel

Brown eyes. Auction price: $12,000. Born April 16, 2013. Buyback donator: Mark Zebley/ Janet Marabito.

Notes:

_____

_____

_____

_____

_____

_____

_____

_____

_____

_____

_____

Gracey

Black Pearl

Pearl
mare   birth year: 2014   brand: 14
SOCKETT TO ME x LEAH'S BAYSIDE ANGEL

Brown eyes. Auction price: $21,000. Buyback donator: Catherine Miller.

Notes:

Black Pearl

Black Pinto

Baybe

Baby
mare   birth year: 2006   brand: none
TUFFER THAN LEATHER X APRIL MOON

Brown eyes. Donated to the CVFD in 2013.

Notes:

_____

_____

_____

_____

_____

_____

_____

_____

_____

_____

_____

Baybe

Black Pinto

Calendar Girl

mare   birth year: 2017   brand: 17
WH Nightwind x (unknown)

Born May 22, 2017.
Donated to CVFC
March 2018. Great
Great Great Grandfoal
of Misty.

Notes:

Calendar Girl

Beach Boy

Saltwater Renegade, Renegade
stallion   birth year: 2015   brand: 15
WH Nightwind x WH Sea Breeze

Brown eyes. Donated to the CVFC August 2015. Great Great Great Grandfoal of Misty.

Notes:

_____

_____

_____

_____

_____

_____

_____

_____

_____

_____

_____

Beach Boy

Buckskin

Alice's Sandcastle

mare   birth year: 2012   brand: 12
NORTH STAR x LIVING LEGEND

Brown eyes. Auction price: $5,300. Born April 27, 2012. Buyback donator: Carol Dennis.

Notes:

Alice's Sandcastle

Buckskin

Anne Bonny's Little Flower

Flower
mare   birth year: 2019   brand: 19
Tornado's Legacy x Anne Bonny

Brown eyes. Auction price: $12,500. First seen June 19, 2019. Buyback donator: Buy Back Babes.

Notes:

_____

_____

_____

_____

_____

_____

_____

_____

_____

_____

_____

Anne Bonny's Little Flower

Buckskin

CLG Rider on the Storm

Rider, Storm
stallion birth year: 2019 brand: 19
TORNADO'S LEGACY x MIRACLE'S NATURAL BEAUTY

Brown eyes. Auction price: $16,500. First seen April 15, 2019. Buyback donator: Chincoteague Legacy Group.

Notes:

_____

_____

_____

_____

_____

_____

_____

_____

_____

_____

_____

CLG Rider on the Storm

Buckskin

Ivana Marie Zustan

Zustan
mare   birth year: 2016   brand: 16
LITTLE DOLPHIN x JESSICA'S SEA STAR SANDY

Brown eye. Auction
price: $5,700. Born May
19, 2016.

Notes:

Ivana Marie Zustan

Jessica's Sea Star Sandy

Jessica's Sandy
mare   birth year: 2006   brand: 06
TORNADO X PHILLY GIRL

Brown eyes. Auction price: $5,300. Born May 17, 2006. Buyback donator: Debbie Elliott-Fisk.

Notes:

_____

_____

_____

_____

_____

_____

_____

_____

_____

_____

_____

Jessica's Sea Star Sandy

Buckskin

Liz's Serenity

Serenity
mare   birth year: 2017   brand: 17
WILD BILL x LANDRIE'S GEORGIA PEACH

Brown eyes. Auction price: $10,000. First seen April 26, 2017. Buyback donator: In memory of Liz Spino by family and friends.

Notes:

Liz's Serenity

Buckskin

Poco Latte PW

mare   birth year: 2002   brand: 02
GUNNER'S MOON x MISTY DAWN

Brown eyes. Auction price: $6,750. Born July 15, 2002.

Notes:

_____

_____

_____

_____

_____

_____

_____

_____

_____

_____

_____

Poco Latte PW

Buckskin

Sunrise Ocean Tides

Sunny
mare   birth year: 2015   brand: 15
LITTLE DOLPHIN X JESSICA'S SEA STAR SANDY

Brown eyes. Auction
price: $3,100. Born
May 29, 2015. Buyback
donator: Lowrey
Family.

Notes:

Sunrise Ocean Tides

Buckskin

Too Grand

Taffee, Salt Water Taffee
mare   birth year: 2000   brand: 00
CINNAMON HOLOGRAM x MERRY TEAPOT'S HIGH BID

Brown eyes. Born July 2000. Alternate sire: North Star. Buyback donator: An elementary school class.

Notes:

_____

_____

_____

_____

_____

_____

_____

_____

_____

_____

_____

_____

Too Grand

Buckskin

Kachina Grand Star

Kachina
mare   birth year: 2005   brand: 05, partial
NORTH STAR x TOO GRAND

Brown eyes. Auction price: $4,000. Born June 3, 2005. Buyback donator: Ginny Zelevitch and Joanne Rome.

Notes:

_____

_____

_____

_____

_____

_____

_____

_____

_____

_____

_____

Kachina Grand Star

Buckskin Comparison Chart

Name	Pg #	Brand	Mane	Face
Alice's Sandcastle	148	12	right	
Anne Bonny's Little Flower	150	19	left	
CLG Rider on the Storm	152	19	right	
Ivana Marie Zustan	154	16	right	
Jessica's Sea Star Sandy	156	06	right	
Kachina Grand Star	166	05, partial	left	star
Liz's Serenity	158	17	right	
Poco Latte PW	160	02	right	
Sunrise Ocean Tides	162	15	right	
Too Grand	164	00	left	

NOTES

Left & right refers to the animal's left & right.

Mane: left = falls to the left **right** = falls to the right **split** = significant portion falls on left and right

Buckskin Comparison Chart

Legs				Notable Details
R F	R B	L F	L B	
				stallion
	sock		sock	
				dark dappled coat

R F = right front   **R B** = right back **L F** = left front   **L B** = left back
sock = white well below the knee   **stocking** = white near and above the knee

baldface = white covers most of the face   **blaze** = white streak running down the length of the face   **snip** = white spot on the muzzle   **star** = white spot on the forehead

Buckskin Pinto

Molly's Rosebud

Rosie
mare   birth year: 2010   brand: none
YANKEE SPIRIT x MERRY TEAPOT'S HIGH BID

Brown eyes. Auction price: $5,800. Born May 4, 2010.

Notes:

_____

_____

_____

_____

_____

_____

_____

_____

_____

_____

_____

Molly's Rosebud

Buckskin Pinto

CLG Bay Princess

Bay Princess
mare   birth year: 2016   brand: 16
Tornado's Prince of Tides x Baybe

Brown eyes. Auction
price: $10,000. First
seen April 22, 2016.
Buyback donator:
Chincoteague Legacy
Group.

Notes:

_____

_____

_____

_____

_____

_____

_____

_____

_____

_____

_____

CLG Bay Princess

Buckskin Pinto

CLG ToMorrow's Tidewater Twist

Twist, Triple T, Tidewater Twist
stallion   birth year: 2017   brand: 17
Tornado's Legacy x Sweetheart

Brown eyes. Auction price: $8,400. First seen March 13, 2017. Buyback donator: Chincoteague Legacy Group.

Notes:

_____

_____

_____

_____

_____

_____

_____

_____

_____

_____

_____

_____

CLG ToMorrow's Tidewater Twist

Buckskin Pinto

Badabing

mare   birth year: 2015   brand: 15
Tornado's Prince of Tides x Ella of Assateague

Brown eyes. Auction
price: $4,500. Born
May 12, 2015. Buyback
donators: Julie Barry,
Yuki Banks, and Linda
Cook.

Notes:

_____

_____

_____

_____

_____

_____

_____

_____

_____

_____

_____

_____

Badabing

Buckskin Pinto

Tornado's Legacy

Legacy, Lil Tornado
stallion   birth year: 2007   brand: 07
Tornado x Unci

Brown eyes. Auction price: $11,000. Born April 3, 2007.

Notes:

_____

_____

_____

_____

_____

_____

_____

_____

_____

_____

_____

Buckskin Pinto

Tornado's Legacy

Buckskin Pinto

Randy

mare   birth year: 2014   brand: 14
TORNADO'S PRINCE OF TIDES X BAYBE

Brown eyes. Auction price: $8,100. Buyback donator: Heckman Family.

Notes:

_____

_____

_____

_____

_____

_____

_____

_____

_____

_____

_____

Randy

Buckskin Pinto

Serendipity

mare   birth year: 2018   brand: 18
MAVERICK x CALCETÍN

Brown eyes. Auction price: $8,200. Alternate sire: Ace's Black Tie Affair. First seen April 29, 2018. Buyback donator: Gina Marabito Zebley.

Notes:

Serendipity

Buckskin Pinto

Tidewater Treasure

Treasure
mare birth year: 2000 brand: none
CHEROKEE CHIEF x BLONDE

Brown eyes. Donated to CVFC December 2018.

Notes:

_____

_____

_____

_____

_____

_____

_____

_____

_____

_____

Tidewater Treasure

Chestnut

JABATAA

mare   birth year: 2002   brand: 02
CHEROKEE CHIEF x ROSIE O' GRADY

Brown eyes. Auction price: $4,900. Born July 2002. Buyback donator: Mauger family.

Notes:

_____

_____

_____

_____

_____

_____

_____

_____

_____

_____

JABATAA

Chestnut

Surfer's Shining Star

Gingersnap
mare   birth year: 2015   brand: 15
SURFER DUDE x TSG's ELUSIVE STAR

Brown eyes. Auction price: $6,500. Born March 23, 2015. Buyback donator: Julie Barry.

Notes:

_____

_____

_____

_____

_____

_____

_____

_____

_____

_____

Surfer's Shining Star

Chestnut

Surfin' Chantel

mare   birth year: 2013   brand: 13
RAINBOW WARRIOR x SURFIN' SCARLET

*Brown eyes. Born
September 2013. Fall
buyback.*

Notes:

_____

_____

_____

_____

_____

_____

_____

_____

_____

_____

_____

Surfin' Chantel

Chestnut

Susana

mare   birth year: 2001   brand: 01
CHEROKEE CHIEF X GLAMOUR GIRL

Brown eyes. Born July 20, 2001. Alternate sire: Surfer Dude. Buyback donator: Strofhoff family.

Notes:

_____

_____

_____

_____

_____

_____

_____

_____

_____

_____

_____

Susana

Chestnut

Suzy's Sweetheart

mare   birth year: 1998   brand: 98
CHEROKEE CHIEF X VOYAGER

Brown eyes. Born July 1998. Alternate sire: Tornado.

Notes:

_____

_____

_____

_____

_____

_____

_____

_____

_____

_____

Suzy's Sweetheart

Chestnut

Sue's Crown of Hope

Hope
mare   birth year: 2019   brand: 19
KEN x KIMMEE-SUE

Brown eyes. Auction price: $1,600. First seen May 14, 2019. Buyback donator: Joe Lowery, In memory of Sue Wingfield Lowery by family and friends.

Notes:

Sue's Crown of Hope

197

Chestnut

Surfin' Scarlet

Scarlet
mare   birth year: 2000   brand: 00
SURFER DUDE X SURF QUEEN

Brown eyes. Born July 2000. Buyback donator: Strand family.

Notes:

_____

_____

_____

_____

_____

_____

_____

_____

_____

_____

_____

Surfin' Scarlet

Chestnut

Tuleta Star

mare   birth year: 2002   brand: 02
CHEROKEE CHIEF x A TOUCH OF DUST

Brown eyes. Auction price: $5,000. Born July 17, 2002. Buyback donator: Tuleta White.

Notes:

_____

_____

_____

_____

_____

_____

_____

_____

_____

_____

Tuleta Star

Chestnut

Cinnamon Blaze

mare   birth year: 1999   brand: unreadable
(UNKNOWN) X SNEAKERS

Brown eyes.

Notes:

_____

_____

_____

_____

_____

_____

_____

_____

_____

_____

Cinnamon Blaze

Chestnut

Kimmee-Sue

mare   birth year: 2012   brand: 12
Courtney's Boy x Cinnamon Blaze

Brown eyes. Auction price: $5,000. Born May 2, 2012. Buyback donator: Sue Fitzgerald.

Notes:

Kimmee-Sue

Chestnut

Precious Jewel

mare   birth year: 2014   brand: 14
PHANTOM MIST x UNCI

Brown eyes. Auction price: $5,200. Buyback donator: Sibyl and Elton Wright.

Notes:

_____

_____

_____

_____

_____

_____

_____

_____

_____

_____

Chestnut

Precious Jewel

207

Chestnut

Unforgettable 2001

Diamond
mare   birth year: 2001   brand: none
HURRICANE x JUST MY STYLE

Brown eyes. Born September 2001. Alternate dam: Glamour Girl.

Notes:

_____

_____

_____

_____

_____

_____

_____

_____

_____

_____

Unforgettable 2001

Chestnut

Judy's Little Smooch

Smooch
mare   birth year: 2016   brand: none
SURFER'S RIPTIDE x BUTTERFLY KISSES

Brown eyes. Born
August 9, 2016.
Buyback donator: Judy
Fuccello.

Notes:

_____

_____

_____

_____

_____

_____

_____

_____

_____

_____

Judy's Little Smooch

Surfer Dude's Gidget

Gidget
mare   birth year: 2002   brand: F, 02, partial

SURFER DUDE X VIRGINIA BELLE

Brown eyes. Auction price: $7,800. Born March 12, 2002. Buyback donator: Buyback Babes.

Notes:

_____

_____

_____

_____

_____

_____

_____

_____

_____

_____

_____

Chestnut

Surfer Dude's Gidget

Chestnut

Dreamer's Gift

mare   birth year: 2012   brand: 12
SURFER DUDE x LYRA'S VEGA

Brown eyes. Auction price: $4,300. Buyback donator: Janey, Anna, and Amanda Beer.

Notes:

_____

_____

_____

_____

_____

_____

_____

_____

_____

_____

_____

Dreamer's Gift

Chestnut

Surfer Princess

mare   birth year: 2015   brand: 15
SURFER DUDE x SURF QUEEN

Brown eyes. Auction price: $5,300. Born May 14, 2015. Buyback donators: Julie Barry, Yuki Banks, and Linda Cook.

Notes:

_____

_____

_____

_____

_____

_____

_____

_____

_____

_____

_____

Surfer Princess

Chestnut

Surfette

mare   birth year: 2017   brand: 17
(UNKNOWN) X SUNDANCE

Brown eyes. Donated to CVFC March 2018. Sired by a Surfer Dude son. Great Great Great Great Grandfoal of Misty.

Notes:

Surfette

Chestnut

Ken

Valentine
stallion   birth year: 2008   brand: 08
WILD THING x STAR GAZER

Brown eyes. Auction price: $4,500. Born February 14, 2008. Alternate sire: Glacier. Buyback donator: Sue Lowery.

Notes:

_____

_____

_____

_____

_____

_____

_____

_____

_____

_____

_____

Ken

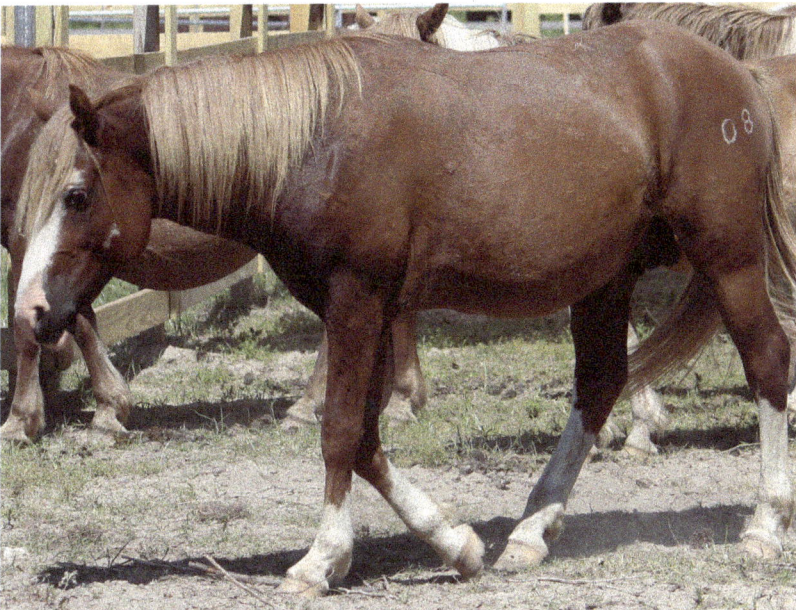

Chestnut

Dreamer's Stardust

Stardust
mare   birth year: 2018   brand: 18
KEN x DREAMER'S GIFT

*Brown eyes. First
seen March 8, 2018.
Buyback donator: Beer
Family.*

Notes:

Dreamer's Stardust

Chestnut

Surfer's Riptide

Riptide
stallion   birth year: 2009   brand: 09, partial
SURFER DUDE x SURF QUEEN

Brown eyes. Auction price: $11,500. Born May 3, 2009. Buyback donator: Folsom family.

Notes:

_____

_____

_____

_____

_____

_____

_____

_____

_____

_____

Surfer's Riptide

Chestnut Comparison Chart

Name	Pg #	Brand	Mane	Face
Cinnamon Blaze	202	unreadable	left	blaze
Dreamer's Gift	214	12	split	star and snip
Dreamer's Stardust	222	18	split	blaze
JABATAA	186	02	right	
Judy's Little Smooch	210		right	blaze
Ken	220	08	left	baldface
Kimmee-Sue	204	12	left	blaze
Precious Jewel	206	14	split	blaze
Sue's Crown of Hope	196	19	right	star
Surfer Dude's Gidget	212	F, 02, partial	split	blaze
Surfer Princess	216	15	right	star and snip
Surfer's Riptide	224	09, partial	right	baldface
Surfer's Shining Star	188	15	right	
Surfette	218	17	right	blaze
Surfin' Chantel	190	13	right	
Surfin' Scarlet	198	00	right	star
Susana	192	01	right	
Suzy's Sweetheart	194	98	right	
Tuleta Star	200	02	right	star and snip
Unforgettable 2001	208		left	star

NOTES

Left & right refers to the animal's left & right.

Mane: left = falls to the left **right** = falls to the right **split** = significant portion falls on left and right

R F = right front **R B** = right back **L F** = left front **L B** = left back
sock = white well below the knee **stocking** = white near and above the knee

226

Chestnut Comparison Chart

Legs				Notable Details
R F	R B	L F	L B	
sock	sock	sock	sock	blond mane & tail
stocking	stocking	stocking	stocking	blond mane & tail
				very dark coat
	stocking			
sock	stocking	sock	stocking	stallion; small white kiss mark on left cheek; blond mane & tail
			sock	
				large crescent shaped star; 1 in brand is smeared
	sock	sock	sock	dark coat; much lighter mane & tail
sock	sock	sock	sock	arrowhead shaped spot on left side
stocking	stocking	stocking	stocking	stallion; dark coat; blond mane & tail; long forelock covers eyes
				dark red coat; mane & tail a little lighter
sock	sock	sock	sock	dark brown
				small whitish diamond-shaped patch on right hip
				small stature
				long forelock
		sock	sock	dark coat

baldface = white covers most of the face   blaze = white streak running down the length of the face   snip = white spot on the muzzle   star = white spot on the forehead

Chestnut Pinto

Catwalk's Olympic Glory

Glory
mare   birth year: 2016   brand: 16
Ajax x Catwalk Chaos

Brown eyes. Auction price: $8,100. Born May 2, 2016. Buyback donator: Leslie Joliet.

Notes:

_____

_____

_____

_____

_____

_____

_____

_____

_____

_____

Catwalk's Olympic Glory

Chestnut Pinto

Chili

Lil Miss Hot Stuff
mare   birth year: 2016   brand: 17, partial
CHIEF GOLDEN EAGLE x CLOUDBURST

Brown eyes. Born September 24, 2016. Donated to CVFC March 2018.

Notes:

_____

_____

_____

_____

_____

_____

_____

_____

_____

_____

_____

Chili

Chestnut Pinto

Slash of White

mare　　　birth year: 1998　brand: 98
WITCH DOCTOR x SWEET MISCHIEF

Brown eyes. Born July 1998.

Notes:

_____
_____
_____
_____
_____
_____
_____

_____
_____
_____
_____

Slash of White

Chestnut Pinto

Lefty's Checkmark

Butterfly
mare   birth year: 2000   brand: none
CHEROKEE CHIEF x RAPT IN PAINT

Brown eyes.

Notes:

_____

_____

_____

_____

_____

_____

_____

_____

_____

_____

_____

Lefty's Checkmark

Chestnut Pinto

CJ SAMM'N

mare   birth year: 2006   brand: 06
NORTH STAR x SLASH OF WHITE

Brown eyes. Auction price: $3,700. Born May 7, 2006. Alternate sire: Leonard Stud.

Notes:

_____

_____

_____

_____

_____

_____

_____

_____

_____

_____

_____

CJ SAMM'N

237

Chestnut Pinto

Kimball's Rainbow Delight

Rainy, Rainbow Delight
mare   birth year: 2006   brand: 06, partial
NORTH STAR X RAMBLING RUBY

Brown eyes. Auction price: $3,100. Born May 9, 2006. Buyback donator: Mary and Normal Kimball.

Notes:

_____

_____

_____

_____

_____

_____

_____

_____

_____

_____

_____

Kimball's Rainbow Delight

Chestnut Pinto

Good Ole Days Bailey's Star

Star
mare   birth year: 2004   brand: none
(UNKNOWN) X (UNKNOWN)

Brown eyes. Donated to CVFC December 2018.

Notes:

_____

_____

_____

_____

_____

_____

_____

_____

_____

_____

_____

Good Ole Days Bailey's Star

Chestnut Pinto

Tiger Lily

Waterbaby
mare   birth year: 2002   brand: none
CHEROKEE CHIEF x VOYAGER

Brown eyes. Born September 2002.

Notes:

_____

_____

_____

_____

_____

_____

_____

_____

_____

_____

Tiger Lily

Chestnut Pinto

Pony Girl's Bliss

Bliss
mare   birth year: 2017   brand: 17
Effie's Papa Bear x Carol's Little Freedom

Brown eyes. Auction price: $7,100. First seen June 4, 2017. Buyback donator: Cassou family.

Notes:

Pony Girl's Bliss

Chestnut Pinto

Susie Q

Lady Hook
mare   birth year: 1996   brand: 96
P<small>REMIERRE</small> x V<small>IXEN</small>

Brown eyes. Auction price: $3,600. Born May 1996.

Notes:

_____

_____

_____

_____

_____

_____

_____

_____

_____

_____

_____

Susie Q

Chestnut Pinto

Catwalk Chaos

Margarita
mare   birth year: 2010   brand: none
CHAOS X PAINT BY NUMBER

Brown eyes. Auction price: $8,100. Born May 8, 2010.

Notes:

_____

_____

_____

_____

_____

_____

_____

_____

_____

_____

Catwalk Chaos

Chestnut Pinto

Carli Marie

mare   birth year: 2018   brand: 18
ACE'S BLACK TIE AFFAIR x GIDGET'S BEACH BABY

Brown eyes. Auction price: $7,000. First seen April 29, 2018.

Notes:

_____

_____

_____

_____

_____

_____

_____

_____

_____

Carli Marie

Chestnut Pinto

Anne Bonny

mare   birth year: 2012 brand: none
YANKEE SPIRIT x MYSTERY

Brown eyes. Auction price: $4,200. Born April 25, 2011. Buyback donator: Sarah Sickles.

Notes:

Anne Bonny

Chestnut Pinto

Sweet Jane

Duckie
mare   birth year: 2006   brand: 06, partial
Courtney's Boy x Lefty's Checkmark

Brown eyes. Auction price: $4,200. Born April 6, 2006. Buyback donator: Sara Rasmussen.

Notes:

Sweet Jane

Chestnut Pinto

Little Duckie

Quackers
mare   birth year: 2011   brand: F
NORTH STAR x SWEET JANE

Brown eyes. Auction price: $3,200. Born May 28, 2011.

Notes:

_____

_____

_____

_____

_____

_____

_____

_____

_____

_____

_____

Little Duckie

Chestnut Pinto

Two Teagues Taco's Chilibean

Chilibean
mare   birth year: 2019   brand: 19
ACE'S BLACK TIE AFFAIR X TWO TEAGUES TACO

Brown eyes. Auction price: $10,500. First seen June 19, 2019. Buyback donator: Buy Back Babes.

Notes:

Two Teagues Taco's Chilibean

Chestnut Pinto

Misty Mills

mare   birth year: 2006   brand: 06, partial
COURTNEY'S BOY x SWEET MISCHIEF

Brown eyes. Auction price: $5,000. Born June 20, 2006.

Notes:

_____

_____

_____

_____

_____

_____

_____

_____

_____

_____

Misty Mills

Chestnut Pinto

Beach Bunny

mare   birth year: 2015   brand: 15
ARCHER'S GAMBIT x SWEET JANE

Brown eyes. Auction price: $6,000. Born May 13, 2015.

Notes:

_____

_____

_____

_____

_____

_____

_____

_____

_____

_____

Beach Bunny

Chestnut Pinto

Archer's Gambit

Puzzle, Little Frog
stallion   birth year: 2008   brand: 08
NORTH STAR x LILY PAD

Brown eyes. Auction price: $5,300. Born April 24, 2008.

Notes:

_____

_____

_____

_____

_____

_____

_____

_____

_____

_____

_____

Archer's Gambit

Chestnut Pinto

Checkers

Giraffe

mare   birth year: 1997   brand: 7, partial

(UNKNOWN) x HITCH HIKER

Brown eyes. Born August 1997. Buyback donator: Fitzgerald family.

Notes:

_____

_____

_____

_____

_____

_____

_____

_____

_____

_____

_____

Checkers

Chestnut Pinto

Stevenson's Dakota Sky

Dakota, Dakota Sky
mare   birth year: 2001   brand: 01
Courtney's Boy x Promise of Summer

Brown eyes. Born July 17, 2001. Buyback donator: Catherine Young.

Notes:

Stevenson's Dakota Sky

Chestnut Pinto

Sunny Skies After The Storm

Sunny Skies
mare   birth year: 2019   brand: 19
ARCHER'S GAMBIT X THUNDERSTORM SKIES

One blue, one brown eye. Auction price: $7,500. First seen April 27, 2019. Buyback donator: Mary and Claire Stiehm.

Notes:

_____

_____

_____

_____

_____

_____

_____

_____

_____

_____

_____

Chestnut Pinto

Sunny Skies After The Storm

Chestnut Pinto

Courtney's Island Dove

Dove
mare   birth year: 2006   brand: unreadable
Courtney's Boy x Salt and Pepper

Brown eyes. Auction price: $2,300. Buyback donator: Joann Rome and Ginny Zlevitch.

Notes:

_____

_____

_____

_____

_____

_____

_____

_____

_____

_____

_____

Courtney's Island Dove

Chestnut Pinto

Little Bit O' Joansie

Joansie
mare   birth year: 2014   brand: 14
Courtney's Boy x Cinnamon Blaze

Brown eyes. Auction price: $7,100.

Notes:

Chestnut Pinto

Little Bit O' Joansie

275

Chestnut Pinto

Don Leonard Stud II

Lenny, Leonard Stud II
stallion   birth year: 2014   brand: 14
PHANTOM MIST x TUNIE

Brown eyes. Auction price: $9,000. Buyback donator: Leonard Family.

Notes:

_____

_____

_____

_____

_____

_____

_____

_____

_____

_____

_____

Don Leonard Stud II

Chestnut Pinto

Mary Read

mare   birth year: 2017   brand: 17
Tornado's Legacy x Anne Bonny

Brown eyes. Auction price: $7,500. First seen March 5, 2017. Buyback donator: Darcy Cole, Allison Dotzel, and Sarah Sickles.

Notes:

_____

_____

_____

_____

_____

_____

_____

_____

_____

_____

_____

Mary Read

Chestnut Pinto

Thetis

mare   birth year: 2001   brand: 01
HOT AIR BALLOON x UNTOUCHABLE

Brown eyes. Born July 19, 2001. Alternate sire: Courtney's Boy.

Notes:

_____

_____

_____

_____

_____

_____

_____

_____

_____

_____

_____

Thetis

Chestnut Pinto

Sonny's Legacy

mare   birth year: 2013   brand: 13
DON LEONARD STUD x SHY ANNE

Brown eyes. Born May 10, 2013. Not auctioned, donated in memory of fireman Sonny Haigh.

Notes:

_____

_____

_____

_____

_____

_____

_____

_____

_____

_____

_____

Sonny's Legacy

Chestnut Pinto

Gidget's Beach Baby

Beach Baby
mare   birth year: 2010   brand: none
NORTH STAR x SURFER DUDE'S GIDGET

Brown eyes. Auction price: $5,500. Born May 13, 2010. Buyback donator: Buyback Babes.

Notes:

_____

_____

_____

_____

_____

_____

_____

_____

_____

_____

_____

Gidget's Beach Baby

Chestnut Pinto

Wildfire

mare   birth year: 2013   brand: none
WH Nightwind x WH Sea Breeze

Brown eyes. Donated
to CVFC March 2018.
Great Great Great
Grandfoal of Misty.

Notes:

_____

_____

_____

_____

_____

_____

_____

_____

_____

_____

_____

Wildfire

Chestnut Pinto

Witch Kraft

Friendly Girl
mare   birth year: 1992   brand: none
(UNKNOWN) X WATERKOLOR

Brown eyes.

Notes:

_____

_____

_____

_____

_____

_____

_____

_____

_____

_____

_____

Witch Kraft

Chestnut Pinto

Thunderstorm Skies

Thunder
mare   birth year: 2013   brand: 13
DON LEONARD STUD x LILY PAD

Brown eyes. Auction price: $4,000. Born May 7, 2013. Buyback donator: Laura and George De Berdt Romilly.

Notes:

_____

_____

_____

_____

_____

_____

_____

_____

_____

_____

Thunderstorm Skies

Chestnut Pinto

CLG Rumor Has It

Rumor
mare   birth year: 2018 brand: 18
Ken x Whisper of Living Legend

One blue eye, one
brown eye. Auction
price: $13,200. First
seen May 9, 2018.
Buyback donator:
Chincoteague Legacy
Group.

Notes:

CLG Rumor Has It

Palomino

Chief Golden Eagle

Chief
stallion   birth year: 2008   brand: 08
Glacier x Beautiful Dreamer

Brown eyes. Auction price: $3,800. Born April 1, 2008. Buyback donator: Joann Rome and Ginny Zlevitch.

Notes:

_____

_____

_____

_____

_____

_____

_____

_____

_____

_____

_____

Chief Golden Eagle

Palomino

Kachina Mayli Mist

Mayli
mare   birth year: 2012 brand: 12
PHANTOM MIST x KACHINA GRAND STAR

Brown eyes. Auction price: $7,000. Born April 3, 2012. Buyback donator: Joanne Rome, Ginny Zelevitch, Lowery Family.

Notes:

_____

_____

_____

_____

_____

_____

_____

_____

_____

_____

Kachina Mayli Mist

Palomino

Shy & Sassy Sweet Lady Suede

Suede
mare   birth year: 2014   brand: 14
CHIEF GOLDEN EAGLE x PONY LADIES' SWEET SURPRISE

Brown eyes. Auction price: $7,000. Buyback donator: Kim Theriault.

Notes:

_____

_____

_____

_____

_____

_____

_____

_____

_____

_____

_____

Shy & Sassy Sweet Lady Suede

Palomino

Two Teague's Golden Girl

Goldie
mare   birth year: 2016   brand: 16
CHIEF GOLDEN EAGLE X TWO TEAGUES TACO

Brown eyes. Auction price: $5,000. First seen May 14, 2016. Buyback donator: Buyback Babes.

Notes:

Two Teague's Golden Girl

Palomino

Miss Admiral Halsey

mare   birth year: 2018   brand: 18
SURFER'S RIPTIDE x KACHINA MAYLI MIST

Brown eyes. Auction price: $10,200. First seen May 1, 2018. Buyback donator: Meredith Wright.

Notes:

Palomino

Miss Admiral Halsey

Palomino Comparison Chart

Name	Pg #	Brand	Mane	Face
Chief Golden Eagle	294	08	left	
Kachina Mayli Mist	296	12	left	
Miss Admiral Halsey	302	18	left	blaze
Shy & Sassy Sweet Lady Suede	298	14	split	
Two Teague's Golden Girl	300	16	left	

NOTES

Left & right refers to the animal's left & right.

Mane: left = falls to the left **right** = falls to the right **split** = significant portion falls on left and right

Palomino Comparison Chart

Legs				Notable Details
R F	R B	L F	L B	
				stallion; long forelock
				pale coat; short hairs stand up along neck like a mohawk
sock	sock	sock	sock	only one with white on face and legs

R F = right front   **R B** = right back **L F** = left front   **L B** = left back
sock = white well below the knee   **stocking** = white near and above the knee

baldface = white covers most of the face   **blaze** = white streak running down the length of the face   **snip** = white spot on the muzzle   **star** = white spot on the forehead

Palomino Pinto

Judy's Sunshine

Wings
mare   birth year: 2018   brand: 18
Tornado's Prince of Tides x Catwalk Chaos

Brown eyes. Auction price: $20,000. First seen March 5, 2018. Buyback donator: Judy Ann White.

Notes:

Judy's Sunshine

Palomino Pinto

Tornado's Prince of Tides

Prince
stallion   birth year: 2007   brand: 07
TORNADO X SAND CHERRY

Brown eyes. Auction
price: $17,500. Born
April 7, 2007. Buyback
donator: Buyback
Babes.

Notes:

_____

_____

_____

_____

_____

_____

_____

_____

_____

_____

Tornado's Prince of Tides

Palomino Pinto

Little Miss Sunshine

Sunshine
mare   birth year: 2015   brand: 15
Tornado's Prince of Tides x Baybe

Brown eyes. Auction price: $5,300. Born July 3, 2015. Buyback donator: Joanne Niland and Nancie Oleynik.

Notes:

_____

_____

_____

_____

_____

_____

_____

_____

_____

_____

_____

Little Miss Sunshine

Palomino Pinto

Whisper of Living Legend

Whisper
mare   birth year: 2000   brand: 00
NORTH STAR x LIVING LEGEND

Brown eyes. Born
July 4, 2000. Buyback
donator: David and
Elizabeth Moore.
Alternate sire:
Rainbow Warrior.

Notes:

_____

_____

_____

_____

_____

_____

_____

_____

_____

_____

_____

_____

Whisper of Living Legend

Palomino Pinto

Jigsaw's Little Miss Skeeter

Skeeter

mare   birth year: 2018 brand: 18

Tornado's Legacy x Cody's Little Jigsaw Puzzle

Brown eyes. Auction price: $11,500. First seen May 4, 2018.

Notes:

Jigsaw's Little Miss Skeeter

Palomino Pinto

Sundance

mare   birth year: unk   brand: none
WH Nightwind x (unknown)

Brown eyes. Donated to CVFC March 2018. Great Great Great Grandfoal of Misty.

Notes:

_____

_____

_____

_____

_____

_____

_____

_____

_____

_____

Sundance

Palomino Pinto

Marina's Marsh Mallow

Marsh Mallow
mare   birth year: 2014   brand: 14
TORNADO'S PRINCE OF TIDES X FIFTEEN FRIENDS OF FRECKLES

Brown eyes. Auction price: $7,000. Buyback donator: Cassou family.

Notes:

_____

_____

_____

_____

_____

_____

_____

_____

_____

_____

_____

Marina's Marsh Mallow

Palomino Pinto

Lorna Dune

mare   birth year: 2013   brand: 13
DON LEONARD STUD x JESSICA'S SEA STAR SANDY

Brown eyes. Auction price: $6,200. Born May 5, 2013. Buyback donator: Kathleen Cahall.

Notes:

Lorna Dune

Close Family Index

In order to save space, the relationship of an entry in this index is identified by font and color.

Color Key

Name - Bold Black
SIRE - Small Caps Blue
DAM - Small Caps Pink
Offspring - Green
Sibling Same Sire - Italics Blue
Sibling Same Dam - Italics Pink
Sibling Same Sire & Dam - Italics Black

322

Close Family Index

323

Close Family Index

Close Family Index

Close Family Index

Close Family Index

Close Family Index

Close Family Index

Close Family Index

Alphabetical Index

Alphabetical Index

Alphabetical Index

Alphabetical Index

Brand Index

Brand Index

Brand Index

www.ingramcontent.com/pod-product-compliance
Lightning Source LLC
Chambersburg PA
CBHW041255040426
42334CB00028BA/3016